Legends of the Yosemite Miwok

Legends of the Yosemite Miwok

Compiled by Frank La Pena, Craig D. Bates and Steven P. Medley

Illustrated by Harry Fonseca

YOSEMITE
ASSOCIATION

Yosemite National Park, California

Second, revised edition.

Yosemite Association
P.O. Box 545
Yosemite National Park, CA 95389

The Yosemite Association is a non-profit, membership organization dedicated to the support of Yosemite National Park. Our publishing program is designed to provide an educational service and to increase the public's understanding of Yosemite's special qualities and needs. To learn more about our activities and other publications, or for information about membership, please write to the address above, or call (209) 379-2646.

Printed in the United States of America

Library of Congress Cataloging-in-Publication Data

La Pena, Frank
Legends of the Yosemite Miwok/compiled by Frank La Pena, Craig D. Bates, and Steven P. Medley; illustrated by Harry Fonseca.--2nd rev. ed.
 p. cm.
Includes bibliographical references.
ISBN 0-939666-57-X: $11.95
1. Miwok Indians--Legends. 2. Indians of North America--California--Yosemite Valley--Legends.
I. Bates, Craig D. II. Medley, Steven P., 1949- . III. Title.
E99.M69L3 1993
398.2'089974--dc20
 93-2158 CIP

Contents

Foreword

As Indian people from the Yosemite area and as members of the American Indian Council of Mariposa County, we are gratified to find that there is so much interest in our Native American culture.

There are many legends and stories of Indian tribes throughout the land. The Indians of Yosemite had many unique and special legends. It is fitting that this collection includes both well-known and obscure legends from the Yosemite area.

We are pleased to know that Frank La Pena helped to select the legends for this book. Frank is a Wintu-Nomptipom Indian from Sacramento, California. Also, we admire the imagery of the drawings that Harry Fonseca has prepared to illustrate the legends.

We would like to express our gratitude to the Yosemite Association for publishing these legends for the public to enjoy and for allowing us to review the contents of this book.

Les James
American Indian Council of Mariposa County

Introduction

The California Indians had a vision of the world which included all swimming, flying, walking and crawling beings. They related to both the physical and non-physical world. All things became familiar, known, and named by the People. The Miwok, in further defining the structure of their world, classified each individual as a land person or a water person.

To name something is to begin to understand it; the idea of "naming" and "belonging" helped explain and order the universe. The natural terrain, because it was part of the Indian world, became identified culturally. Like other groups, the American Indian labeled places, villages, towns, and other landmarks, with distinct names.

A major difference between the non-Indian and the Indian is in the way many Indians have related to the land. In stories about the land and creatures of nature, geographic features like springs or rocks (and their place names) mark the locations of special or memorable events. These locations become intimately connected to particular legends or historic incidents. The stories explain the appearance of faces, figures, shapes, designs and animal forms that sometimes are found at these spots. Legends not only describe how a particular place was created and by whom, but they explain why the world and its unique landscape came to appear as they do.

Through myths and legends, anything that existed in the natural world could be "sung" or told about from the beginning of time and creation. Both the physical and the non-physical (or spiritual) worlds could be explained in this way. The objective and the subjective, as manifested in the material and spiritual worlds, combined in the Native vision, and helped bring meaning to existence.

Myths and legends also translated abstract concepts like life and death into more personal terms. So-called "life" stories helped the listener to better comprehend the existence of otherwise mystifying natural forces. Further, it was the role of such stories to pass along traditions and culture. In this way, legends served as transmitters of cultural heritage.

Unfortunately, the death of many storytellers, religious leaders, singers and dancers in the conflicts of the mid-nineteenth century interrupted the oral tradition of Native Americans in California. By the early part of the twentieth century, many native people adopted Anglo lifestyles, and fewer of the young people took time to learn the old ways. Still, some listened to their elders telling the ancient tales – stories of a world unfamiliar to most of us.

This extensively revised edition of *Legends of the Yosemite Miwok* represents an effort first to identify, to the extent literature and history allow, those Yosemite area legends that can be traced to native tellers, and then to reproduce them in a form as close to the original as possible. Whenever there has been a choice, the earliest version of a legend has been used.

In working to accomplish these goals, the compilers have relied heavily on information provided by Native Americans like Agnes Castro and Julia Parker, and on the writings of several anthropologists and others who, over

the years, have recorded stories told by Indians from the Yosemite region. While we might wish that there was more source material available, there has been a remarkable amount of information passed down to us.

Selecting the legends for inclusion in this volume proved difficult. During our research we found that once a given legend appeared in print, it became accepted as authentic (no matter what its origin), and, in several instances, was reprinted many times. This was true for fictional, romanticized legends, as well as for those we consider to be "legitimate." Oftentimes, we came across legends that had been copied verbatim from earlier works.

When we refer to an "authentic" or "legitimate" legend, we use those terms to indicate that the story originated with some certainty from a Native American narrator, and that it was not fabricated by a non-Indian. This does not suggest that there were and are not different versions for a given legend. In fact, for some stories there are as many distinctive forms as there are tellers.

Myths changed as they were re-told, as they were passed from group to group, and as the conditions of native life were altered. Further, a good story teller would flesh out a skeletal legend with vivid details and elaborations which might change with each telling. He or she also would have used the common device of repeating certain story elements. For this reason, the legends reproduced here would have been much longer when presented orally.

Ironically, the first published Yosemite legend was undoubtedly concocted by a Euro-American. It appeared in James Mason Hutchings' *Hutchings' California Magazine* (Vol. IV No. 5, November, 1859) and was reportedly first told in "an eastern journal" by a Yosemite resident known

as "Iota" (probably Stephen Cunningham) who received it from the "lips of an old Indian." Hutchings, who considered it very entertaining, immortalized "The Legend of Tu-tock-ah-nu-lah and Tis-sa-ack" in 1860 when he included it in his book, *Scenes of Wonder and Curiosity in California*. No other versions of the legend were noted thereafter, and no Miwok ever verified the tale. Nonetheless, Hutchings' account has appeared since in a variety of publications. It is not included in this collection of legends.

In 1877, Stephen Powers published a study of the Yosemite Indians as part of his work entitled *Tribes of California*. His renditions of the "Legend of Tu-tok-a-nu'-la" and the "Legend of Tis-se'-yak" (as told by Choko or "Old Jim") were probably the first, genuine Yosemite legends related by a Yosemite Miwok to be published without change or embellishment.

Following Powers, anthropologists C. Hart Merriam, Samuel A. Barrett, Edward W. Gifford, and Alfred L. Kroeber worked in Yosemite, collecting and recording native Miwok myths and legends. All but Merriam were affiliated with the University of California, and the majority of their work relative to this volume was published as part of the series known as the *University of California Publications in American Archaeology and Ethnology*. Disappointingly, they rarely mentioned the names of the Indian people from whom they learned.

The most comprehensive work to result from their studies was *The Dawn of the World: Myths and Weird Tales Told by the Mewan Indians of California* by C. Hart Merriam. Merriam worked with a number of Yosemite Miwok people including Captain Paul, his daughter Julia, and Pete Hilliard in 1902, and Frank Georgely, Captain Dick, Sally Ann Castagnetto, Lena Brown, and Laura Ann in 1910. *Dawn of the World* was used more than any

other volume as a wellhead for this collection, and it is recommended for those who wish to learn more of Miwok mythology.

Another significant body of information was amassed by Frank F. Latta, a school teacher and amateur anthropologist from the Bakersfield area who developed a passion for the myths and legends of the Indians of Central California. His book entitled *California Indian Folklore* contains several Yosemite Miwok stories which were related to him by Chris "Chief Le-Mee" Brown, Maria Lebrado Ydrte and Henry Johnson.

Because the legends included here have come from such a variety of sources, the compilers have made minor changes in style and spelling in an attempt to achieve a consistent treatment throughout. The Miwok name for each character appears only once in each legend so that the text is more readable and less choppy; we have spelled such names as they appear in Merriam's *Dawn of the World* whenever spelling variations have been encountered (unless otherwise noted).

It has been our objective in undertaking this revision to make the contents of this book more historically representative and accurate. If we have succeeded, these legends should better convey the richness of the culture of the Yosemite Miwok people while allowing insights on human nature generally. More than anything else, we hope that our readers will find these legends to be timeless and entertaining stories that are a pleasure to read and hear.

Frank La Pena, Craig D. Bates, and Steven P. Medley

Ū-wū'-lin, the Giant of Ah-wah'-nee

When the first bird and animal people inhabited the Valley of Ah-wah'-nee, it was a time of plenty, and they lived well. Then a great cannibal giant, Ū-wū'-lin, appeared in the north and began to eat the people. He was very hungry. He traveled all over the world and ate nearly every being on earth.

The giant was enormous, as big as a pine tree. His hands were so large that he could hold ten men at a time between his fingers. He went about with a great hunting sack on his back in which he placed his prey. His sack was so large that it would hold all the people of a village at once.

The bird and animal people tried in every way to kill the giant. Nothing they could do would hurt him. Their arrows glanced from his body, and their spears were broken against his huge sides. The giant had neither brain nor blood nor ordinary heart. His heart was located in a tiny spot in his heel, and it was his only point of weakness. The bird and animal people, however, did not know where to find it.

The few people who were still left in the world met to discuss how they might be rid of the giant. They asked Fly, who had a terrible bite, if he might help. Fly went out to search for the giant, and found him asleep. Beginning at the giant's head, Fly traveled over every part of the huge body, biting the giant everywhere. The giant gave no indication that he felt Fly's bites until his heel was reached. When Fly bit the giant's heel, he

kicked his massive leg. Fly knew he had found the giant's weak spot.

Excitedly, Fly returned to the remaining bird and animal people and announced his discovery. Once again they discussed how they might kill the giant. It was decided that they should make a large number of long, sharply-pointed awls. They placed the sharpened stakes all along the trail traveled by the giant. The awls were arranged so that the giant could not walk the trail without their sticking into his feet.

When the giant came down the trail, he stepped on many of the awls. Finally, one of them pierced the heart in his foot. The giant died immediately. In this way, peace was restored to the Valley of Ah-wah'-nee.

Yel'-lo-kin, the Man-Eating Giant

Yel'-lo-kin was a giant bird – the biggest bird in the world. He was in the habit of carrying off children – boys and girls up to fourteen years of age. He grabbed them by the tops of their heads and carried them up through the hole in the middle of the sky. Yel'-lo-kin's home was on top of the sky, and there he killed and ate the children.

Yel'-lo-kin's wife was Ol'-lus muk-ki'-e, the Toad-woman, aunt of We'-pi-ahk, the Eagle. Yel'-lo-kin had stolen her from the earth and had taken her up to his house above the sky. He did not kill her but kept her as his wife. He brought her people to eat, but she would not eat them.

One day Yel'-lo-kin caught Eagle by the top of the head and carried him up through the hole in the sky.

A boy playing saw Yel'-lo-kin catch Eagle and shouted to the people who got poles and bows and arrows and tried to reach Yel'-lo-kin. They could not, and Yel'-lo-kin went on up with Eagle and took him to his house on top of the sky and left him. When Eagle looked around he saw his aunt, Toad-woman. She told him to look out, that in a little while Yel'-lo-kin would come back and kill him. "He will take you to a big tank of blood and ask if you want to drink," she said. "When he does this you must answer 'yes' and pretend to reach down, and tell him the blood is too low, you can't reach it; you are afraid of falling in. Ask him to show you how to get it."

"All right," answered Eagle; he would do as she said.

Then Toad-woman gave him a big stone knife with which to cut off Yel'-lo-kin's head.

Soon Yel'-lo-kin returned and did exactly as his wife said he would do. When he asked Eagle to drink, Eagle told him he could not reach the blood; he was afraid of falling in, and asked Yel'-lo-kin to show him how. When Yel'-lo-kin leaned over and reached down deep in the tank, Eagle struck him with the big knife, cutting off his head. Yel'-lo-kin banged around inside the tank, flapped his big wings, made a great noise, and finally flopped out and died. His stretched out wings were as big as pine trees. Eagle was free.

Ah-hā'-le, the Coyote, was down below. Eagle was his uncle. Coyote asked the people, "Where is my uncle, Eagle?"

The boys told him that Eagle had gone up, that Yel'-lo-kin had carried him up through the sky. Coyote looked but could not see the hole they had gone through. Then he went south and looked for the south hole in the sky, but he could not find it. Returning, he went north to the hole at Thunder Mountain, but could not get in that way for it was too cold. Coyote came back to the village and sprang up high in the air and passed through the middle hole in the sky. It was the same hole that Yel'-lo-kin had gone through with Eagle.

At the very moment Coyote arrived, Eagle struck Yel'-lo-kin with the knife and killed him, and Coyote saw him die.

"It is a good thing that you killed him," Coyote said.

Eagle replied, "He has been stealing our children; whenever he was hungry he went down and got a boy or a girl. We lost many people."

Then Eagle showed Coyote the tank of blood where Yel'-lo-kin had done his killing.

After a while Coyote asked, "What are you going to do with Yel'-lo-kin?"

Eagle said he was going to burn him, so he would not come to life again.

But Coyote replied, "No uncle, you had better not burn him."

Then Eagle asked, "What are you going to do with him?"

Coyote answered, "I think I will cut off his wings and take them down home."

"What will you do with the wings?" asked Eagle.

Coyote replied, "I am going to plant the big feathers and grow trees and other greenery. If I plant plenty of feathers and everything's green, there will be many people. When I am done planting trees, I am going to make people."

When he had finished speaking, Coyote went down to the earth through a hole of his own, for he was a witch doctor.

After Coyote had left, Yel'-lo-kin's wife, Toad-woman, asked Eagle how he was going to get down.

"I do not know," answered Eagle.

"I will take you down," said Toad-woman.

"How?" asked Eagle.

"You will see how," she replied. And she gathered the strong green sword-grass that grows by the river, and made a long rope of it. With it Toad-woman lowered Eagle down to the earth.

Coyote planted the feathers from Yel'-lo-kin's wings, and when they had

come up, he watched them grow. Some grew into grasses, wild oats, flowers, manzanitas, and other bushes. Others grew into yellow pines, sugar pines, black oaks, blue oaks, and other kinds of trees. Coyote told them all to bear seed every year so the people who were coming would have plenty to eat. He also made rivers and rocks. Coyote turned Yel'-lo-kin's heart into a black rock.

When Coyote had done these things he made people. To do so, he planted more feathers. The people multiplied, and in a short time their villages were everywhere in the land.

How Kah'-kool the Raven Became
A Great Hunter

A long time ago, Too'-le the Evening Star and He-le'-jah the Mountain Lion lived together in a cave home. They were chiefs and partners and had a room on the north side of the cave.

They used to send out hunters for meat. One of these, Kah'-kool the Raven, complained to Evening Star and Mountain Lion that he could not come near enough to game to shoot. Because he was white the animals saw him too easily. So Raven decided to make himself black. He took some charcoal and mashed it in a basket and rubbed it all over his body wherever he could reach. He had the others help put it on his back where he could not reach. When Raven was black all over, he went hunting and killed two or three animals the first day, for now they could not see him.

One day Raven went to Big Meadows and climbed on top of Pilot Peak. When the moon rose, he saw away in the east animals with two big ears standing up. He had never seen anything like them before and ran back to the cave and told the chiefs. Raven said the animal must be very big and very wild, for it turned its big ears every way. He wanted to see it.

Every evening Raven went back to the peak and saw the ears in the east, and each time they were a little nearer. But he did not yet know what the animal was. Then Raven went again and this time the ears were only two or three miles away, and he ran back quickly and told the chiefs that the new animals were coming. They were deer coming over the mountains

from the east. They had never visited Raven's territory before.

The next morning Raven went out and for the first time in his life saw a group of deer. He did not know what they were. He saw that they stepped quickly, and that some of them had horns. So he ran back and told Evening Star and Mountain Lion what he had seen, and said that the new animals looked good to eat and he wanted to kill one.

"All right," answered the chiefs. "If you see one in our territory, go ahead and kill him."

So the next morning Raven again went out, and because he was black, the animals came much nearer and were quite close. He hid behind a tree and they came still nearer. Raven picked out a big one and shot his arrow into it and killed it, for he wanted to try the meat. He watched it kick and roll over and die. Raven then went back and told the chiefs that he had killed one and wanted two men to go with him and fetch it. The chiefs sent two men with him, but when they got there they had nothing to cut it with and had to carry the animal home whole. One took it by the front feet, the other by the hind feet. They carried it to the cave and showed it to the chiefs.

Mountain Lion said it was a deer and was good to eat, and told the people to skin it. They did so and ate it all at one meal.

Next morning Raven returned alone to the same place and followed the tracks and soon found the deer. He hid behind a tree and shot one. The others ran, but he shot his arrows so quickly that the deer made only a few jumps before he had killed five, enough for all the people. Raven did not want to kill all. He wanted to leave some bucks and does so there would be more.

This time the chiefs sent five men with Raven. They took flint knives and skinned the deer and carried home all the meat and intestines for supper and breakfast.

Chief Evening Star told Raven that he wanted to see how the deer walked, and would hunt with him. Raven replied that Evening Star was too light, too shiny, and would scare the deer. Evening Star said he would hide behind a tree and not show himself. So he went, and Raven kept him behind. But Evening Star was so bright that the deer saw him and ran away. Evening Star said, "What am I going to do?" Raven made no answer. He was angry because he had to go home without any meat.

Next morning Evening Star went again. He said he was smart and knew what to do. The deer had made a trail. Evening Star dug a hole by the trail and covered up all but his eye with leaves, and thought that when the deer came he would catch one by the foot. But when the deer came they saw his eye shine and ran away.

Then Evening Star said, "I am going to black myself with charcoal, the same as Raven did." He tried, but the charcoal would not stick. He was too bright. He said, "I don't know what to do. I want to kill one or two deer." Then he tried again and mashed more charcoal and put it on thick. The others helped Evening Star and finally made him black all over. Evening Star did not know that the deer could smell him, and again hid on the trail. The deer came again. This time the doe was ahead, the buck behind. The doe smelled him and jumped over him. The buck smelled him and ran back. This discouraged Evening Star so much that he did not know what to do, and he gave up hunting and stayed at home.

Raven, who had become a great hunter, began to hunt again. He went

every morning alone and killed five or ten deer. The people ate the meat and intestines and all, but did not have enough. So Raven worked harder. He started very early in the morning, before daylight, and killed twelve to fifteen deer every day. This was too much for Raven, and before long he took sick and could not hunt at all.

Then the chiefs and all the others had nothing to eat and did not know what to do. Evening Star asked Mountain Lion, and Mountain Lion asked Evening Star, what they should do. Mountain Lion said he would stay and kill his own deer and eat the liver only, not the meat, and would eat it raw. Evening Star said he would go up into the sky and stay there and shine each night. And each did as he had said. Raven has retained his black color to this day.

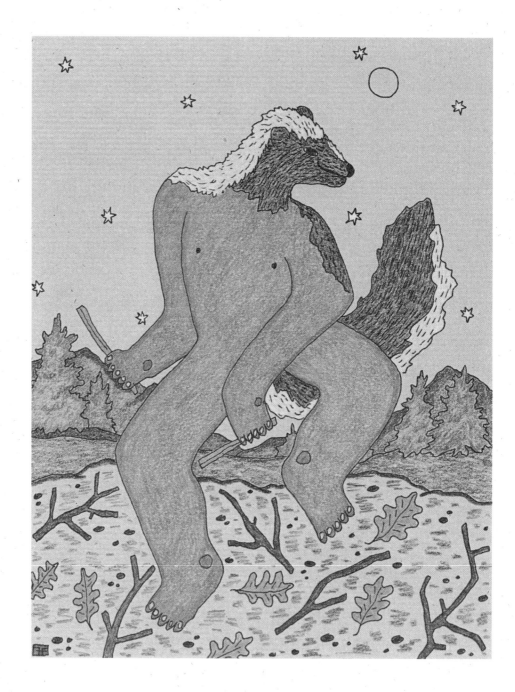

The Greed of His'-sik the Skunk

His'-sik the Skunk and his wife had a daughter who, when she grew up, married Yu'-wel the Gray Fox. Gray Fox was a good hunter, and he and Skunk, who was chief, often hunted together.

Not far from Skunk's home were two high hills standing side by side. In the narrow gap between them ran the trail of So'-koi the elk. One day Skunk told Gray Fox to hide in this narrow place while he went down to the plain to drive up the elk. So Gray Fox hid there and Skunk went down near the elk and fired his terrible scent. The elk could not stand the smell and ran up the trail. Gray Fox waited until the leader and all the others had passed between the hills, and when the last one had gone by he stepped behind them and fired his arrow with such force that it shot through the whole band of elk, killing them all.

When Skunk arrived at the scene he was so glad that he danced. He called all the people to come and help carry the meat home. Then he said to Gray Fox, "You must pack one elk and pack me too, for I am too tired to walk."

Gray Fox was afraid of Skunk and so did as he was told. He lifted a big elk on his shoulders and Skunk climbed up on top. Skunk danced on the body of the elk all the way back to the village.

Then Skunk told the people to skin the elk, and promised them some of the meat. They skinned the elk and cut the meat in strips and hung it up

to dry. When they had done this they asked him for their share. Skunk refused to give them any but told them that they might eat acorn mush and pinole. He then turned as if he were going to shoot his scent, and everyone was afraid.

Skunk was so greedy that he would not give any of the meat to anyone, not even to his own wife and daughter nor to his son-in-law who killed it. He put it all away to dry for himself.

The next day he told Gray Fox to hunt again, and they did the same as before. When the elk were in the narrow pass between the hills, Gray Fox shot his arrow and killed them all, as before.

Then Skunk called the people to come and carry the elk home, and made Gray Fox carry one, and he danced on top on the way, as before.

Again he told the people to skin the elk and he would give them meat for supper. But when they had skinned the elk and cut up the meat, he told them to eat acorns and pinole, at the same time turning to frighten them. Skunk took all the meat to dry for himself, just as he had done before.

The people were very angry, but were afraid to do anything for fear Skunk would shoot his scent and kill them. They talked the matter over for a long time and finally a wise man said, "What are we going to do? Must we hunt for him and pack his meat and skin it for him always, and not get any? We had better kill him, but how can we do it so he will not shoot his scent and kill us?"

Then Too'-wik the Badger spoke. He said, "We can kill him." And while Skunk was watching his meat so that no one could take any of it, Badger dug a big hole and built a fire in it.

Someone asked him why he had made the fire. Badger replied, "Do

you not know that Skunk is a great dancer and loves to dance? We will have fire in the hole, and cover the top over with sticks and leaves and earth so he can't see anything. Then we will send for him to come and dance, and when he dances he will break through and fall in and we shall kill him."

The people answered, "All right."

When it was dark they sent a messenger to Skunk. He said, "You are a great dancer. We want a dance tonight and will pay you well if you will come."

Skunk was pleased and answered, "All right, where shall I dance?"

They took him to the place and, pointing to it, said, "Right here."

Skunk began to dance and sing. Everyone said, "Good, you are doing well. Keep on, you are doing finely. Go ahead, you surely are a great dancer." And they flattered him, and he kept on and danced harder and harder, for he was proud and wanted to show what he could do.

After a while, when Skunk was dancing hardest, the sticks broke and he fell into the hole. The people were ready. They had a very big rock which it had taken many people to bring. They were waiting, and the moment Skunk fell in they pushed the rock quickly over the hole and held it down. They all climbed up on it and held it down tight so Skunk could not get out.

The hot coals burnt Skunk's feet and made him dance. He was very angry and shot his scent so hard against the side of the hole that he pushed mountains up on that side. Then he turned the other way and shot again and pushed mountains up on that side, too. After this his scent was gone, and the coals burnt him and killed him. Then all the people were happy.

The next day the people had a great feast and ate all the dried elk meat they wanted.

How Ah-hā'-le Created People

A long time ago the earth was covered by water and inhabited only by mammal and bird people. Ah-hā'-le, the Coyote, told Frog that he had decided to create people and food for them to eat.

Frog said, "This is all very well, to create all kinds of things, but what good will that do while there is nothing but water here? How can your people live without land?"

Coyote made a plan. He looked for the best diver of all the animals. First he said to Hi'lkūhnai, the small, blue duck, "Dive and see if you can not find some dirt." Duck dived, but he could not find dirt. Two other kinds of ducks tried, too, and so did Watersnake. None of them could find dirt for Coyote. Finally, Frog tried. He dived, and when he returned he held two handfuls of sand high above his head. As Frog surfaced, Coyote called, "Take care, do not drop that." Coyote then scattered sand all around and thus made land upon which his people could live.

Coyote planted all kinds of seeds to make food such as pine nuts, acorns, and others. He wondered what good these food plants would be if there was no one on earth to use them. So he gathered about him half a dozen wise animal people and talked things over with them.

Coyote said, "I have decided to make some good people in this country." The others asked what kind he intended to make. Coyote replied, "I do not know exactly, but I am sure I can make them in some way. You see

we have many kinds of food like pine nuts and acorns, so we must make some people to use them." The others suggested that Coyote create people at once, and he agreed to do so.

He said, "Do you see my foot? Do you think people could use a foot like that?"

"No," replied Waterdog, "look at mine."

Coyote said, "Well, yours is the same as mine; both are round."

Then Pe-ta'-le, the Lizard, spoke up, "Your feet are certainly too round. How can people pick up all kinds of foods if they have feet like yours? Now look at my foot. It has five toes so that I can pick up anything, shoot the bow and arrow, and do many useful things easily."

Coyote answered, "You are right; yours is the proper kind of foot. I shall make people and place them all over the world. Their villages shall be only a little apart, there will be so many of them. I shall arrange it so that each man shall have a wife."

"All right," said Lizard, "you know how to make them, so go ahead."

So Coyote made many people, placing both men and women in villages very close together. Lizard asked why Coyote had placed the men and women together. Coyote replied that in this way each pair should produce a child each year and thereby increase the population. Coyote added that this was to be the last act of creation, and that they could now be content with their work. Thus did Coyote create the people with hands and feet like Lizard's, and send them off to places in every direction.

Coyote then said to Frog, "You like the water. You shall continue to live in the water hereafter." Thus he spoke to each of the animal people and

designated what form each should have and where each should live there-after. When he had finished he said, "You shall all be animals as I have designated. I shall be Coyote and travel about at night in search of my food. There shall be good people living here after this."

How Ah-hā'-le Stole the Sun for the Valley People

To-to'-kan-no, the Sandhill Crane, was chief of the Valley People, and Ah-hā'-le, the Coyote, lived with him. In those times the sun and moon did not shine west of the timber line along the foothills of the Sierra Nevada. In the west, everything was dark and full of fog. There were no regular foods and no baskets or other utensils. People were never married and no children were born. Everything was different.

Coyote was discontented and traveled all about, trying to find a better place for the people. After a while he came to the Foothills Country where it began to be light. He went on a little farther and for the first time in his life saw trees, and found the country dry and warm and good to look at. Soon he saw the Foothills People and found their village. Coyote was himself a magician or witch doctor, so he turned himself into one of the Foothills People and mingled with them. He saw that they had fire, which made light and became the Sun. Coyote saw also that there were both men and women, that the women pounded acorns and cooked acorn mush in baskets, and that everybody ate food. He ate with them and learned that food was good.

When his belly was full, Coyote went home and told Sandhill Crane that he had found a good place where there were people who had the sun and moon and stars, and women, and things to eat. He then asked Sandhill Crane, "What are we going to do? Are we going to stay down

here in the dark and never eat? The people up there have wives and children; the women make acorn soup and other things; the men have light and can see to hunt and kill deer. We live down here in the dark and have no women and nothing to eat. What are we going to do?"

Sandhill Crane answered, "Those things are not worth having. I do not want the sun, nor the light, nor any of those things. Go back up there if you want to."

Coyote went back to the foothills and did as he had done before. He liked the country and the people. Then Coyote returned and told Sandhill Crane what he had told him before. Again he asked, "What are we going to do? Can't we buy the sun? The people up there send the sun away nights so they can sleep, and it comes back every day so they can see to hunt and get things to eat and have a good time. I like the sun. Let us buy him."

Sandhill Crane answered, "What is the matter with you? What would you do with the sun? How would you use it?" Coyote replied, "I do not know exactly, but we would manage in some way to make it go."

Coyote went back to the Foothills People several times, and the more he saw of the sun, the more he wanted it. No one believed his story and some even openly made fun of him, calling him a wild dreamer. And still Sandhill Crane said he did not want the sun. Finally, however, he told Coyote that he might go and find out what the sun would cost.

Coyote went and found that the people would not sell it. If he wanted the sun, he would have to steal it. This would be very difficult because Ah-wahn'-dah the Turtle, keeper of the sun, was very watchful. He slept only a few minutes at a time and then stood up and looked around. Besides,

when Turtle slept, he always kept one eye open. If Coyote moved his foot, Turtle would pick up his bow and arrow. Coyote felt discouraged and did not know what to do. He feared that in order to get the sun he would have to take Turtle, also.

Coyote decided to try once more, so he went again and turned into a man of the Foothills People. Late in the afternoon, all the hunters went off to hunt deer. Then Coyote turned himself into a big oak limb and fell down on the trail. He hoped that Turtle, the sun's keeper, would come along first. And so it happened, for soon Turtle came along the trail, saw the crooked limb, picked it up, carried it home on his shoulder, and threw it down on the ground. After supper he picked it up again and threw it against the fire, but it would not lay flat for it was very crooked and always turned up. Finally, Turtle threw the limb right into the middle of the fire. Coyote, who was now in the fire, did not burn, but kept perfectly still and wished the keeper, Turtle, would go to sleep.

Soon this happened and Turtle fell fast asleep. Then Coyote changed back into his own form, seized the sun, and ran quickly away with it.

Turtle awoke and saw that the sun was gone and called everybody to come quick and find it. But they could not for Coyote had taken it down through the fog to the Valley People, and they dared not venture further on account of the darkness.

But when the Valley People saw the sun they were afraid and turned away from it, for it was too bright and hurt their eyes. They feared that they could never sleep.

Coyote took it to the chief, Sandhill Crane, but he would not have it. He said he didn't understand it and that Coyote must make the sun go,

just as the Foothills People had done it.

When Sandhill Crane refused to have anything to do with the sun, Coyote was disappointed, for he had worked very hard to get it.

Still he said, "Well, I will make it go."

So Coyote arranged it so that the sun moved as it does now. He carried the sun west to the place where the sky comes down to the earth, and found the west hole in the sky. Coyote told the sun to go through the hole and down under the earth and come up on the east side and climb up through the east hole in the sky. He instructed the sun to make light over the Foothills People first, then to continue down and make light over the Valley People. Next, sun was to go through the west hole again and back under the earth so the people could sleep, and to keep doing this, traveling all the time.

The sun did as he was told. Then Sandhill Crane and the Valley People were glad, because they could see to hunt. The Foothills People were satisfied, too, for they had the light in the daytime so they could see, and at night the sun went away so all the people could sleep.

How Meadowlark Started Death

When the first person died, Ah-hā'-le, the Coyote, was to the south of him. Meadowlark was to the north. Before long, the body of the dead person began to stink. Meadowlark smelled it, and he did not like the strong stench. Coyote, who had much power, said to Meadowlark, "I think I will make him get up." Meadowlark replied, "No, do not. If he gets up again, there will be too many people. They will become so hungry that they will eat each other."

Coyote said, "That is not so bad. I do not like people to die." But Meadowlark told him, "No, it is not well to have too many. There will be others to replace those that die. A man will have many children. The old people will die, but the young will live."

Then Coyote said nothing more. So from that time on, people have always died.

Coyote said, "It will be best to put the dead into the fire." And since then, the dead have been burned.

Tim-me-lā'-le the Thunder

When Ū-wū'-lin the giant was traveling over the country eating people, there were two little boys, brothers, who were out hunting when the giant visited their village, and so escaped. When they came home they found that their father and mother and all the other people had been killed and eaten.

The younger boy asked the other, "What shall we do? Shall we live here, just the two of us? Maybe you are clever enough to turn into some other kind of thing and never die."

The elder brother did not know. He was stupid. The younger was the bright one.

For about a month they hunted birds and ate them. One day they made a little hut by a spring where the birds came to drink. Here they killed a great many birds of different kinds.

The younger brother said, "Let us save all the feathers of the birds we kill, wing feathers, tail feathers, and all."

Soon they had enough for both, and the younger said, "We have enough. Let us be big birds and never grow old or die."

"How are we to do it?" asked the elder brother.

The younger answered, "You know how the big birds spread their wings and go, without bothering to eat or drink."

They took the big wing feathers they had saved and stuck them in a

row along their arms, and soon had wings. Then they stuck other feathers all over their bodies and soon were covered like big birds.

Then the younger brother said, "You fly. Let me see you fly a little way." The elder brother tried but could not make his wings go.

"Try again and I will help," said the younger, and he pushed his brother along. But though he tried again, he could not fly and dropped down.

Then they took more feathers and set them closer so they would not leak air. When they had done this the younger asked, "Do you think you can go this time?"

But the elder one replied, "Let me see you try."

"All right," the younger answered, and flew a little way.

"Now you try," he called, and lifted his brother up and pushed him to help him start. But when the elder had flown a little way he cried out that he could not go any farther.

"Go on, I am coming," called the younger. He soon caught up and came under his brother and sailed round and round and went up into the air and came down.

Then the younger said, "Now we can fly, what kind of animal shall we be?"

The elder answered that he did not know.

The younger said, "How about We-ho'-whe-mah the waterbird?"

"All right," replied the other. So they flew again up and down and around.

After awhile, the younger again asked his brother if he would like to be a water bird.

The brother replied, "No, I don't want to live on the water."

"Then how would you like to be Tim-me-lā'-le the Thunder?" asked the younger. "We could come back sometimes and make a big noise and frighten the people. In summer we could go up through the north hole in the sky and stay above it. In winter we could come back here and make a big noise and rain to make the country green. Then maybe the people would come back and live again. We once had a father and mother and sister and uncle and grandfather and others. Maybe they would come back. We want to help them. We could make good rain to make things grow, like acorns, pine nuts, grass and all. Then maybe the people would come back and eat. We should never use food, never drink water, never grow old, and never be killed."

"All right," answered the elder. "We shall live always. But how are we going to make rain?"

"I will show you," replied the younger. And they started again and went up very slowly, way up to the sky, and went north and found the north hole and went through it. When near the sky, but before they had gone through, the younger began to make a loud rumbling noise; it was Thunder. The elder tried but failed. The younger told him to try again. He did so and in a short time was able to make rolling Thunder quite well. Then they went through the hole and up above the sky.

When winter came the younger said, "Come, let us go back." So they came down through the hole in the sky and traveled south and saw that people were there already. Then they shouted and made thunder and rain. Afterwards they returned home through the north sky hole. And every winter even to this day they come back and thunder and make rain to grow things for the people.

The Legend of Tu-tok-a-nu'-la

Long ago two little bear cubs living in the Valley of Ah-wah'-nee went down to the river to swim. They paddled and splashed about to their hearts' content. The cubs then returned to shore and climbed up on a huge boulder that stood beside the water. They lay down to dry themselves in the warm sunshine, and very soon they fell asleep.

The bear cubs slept so soundly that they did not awaken. Through sleeps, moons and snows, both winter and summer, they slumbered on.

Meanwhile, the great rock upon which they slept began to rise. It rose day and night, little by little, until it had lifted them up high into the sky. In this way the cubs were carried out of sight and beyond voice of their bird and animal friends below. They were lifted up into the blue heavens, far up, far up, until the little bears scraped their faces against the moon. Still they slumbered and slept year after year, safe among the clouds.

The bird and animal people of Ah-wah'-nee missed the bear cubs, and cried for them. One day they all assembled together in the hope of bringing down the little bears from the top of the great rock. One at a time, each animal made a spring up the face of the wall as far as he could leap.

The little mouse could only jump up the breadth of a hand. The rat jumped two handbreadths, and the raccoon made it little further. The grizzly bear made a mighty leap far up the wall, but fell back in vain like all the others. Last of all, the mountain lion tried, and he jumped up fur-

ther than any other animal. But he, too, fell flat on his back.

Then along came Tul-tak-a-na, an insignificant measuring worm, which even the mouse could crush with his foot. The measuring worm began to creep up the rock. Step by step, a little at a time, he measured his way up. Before long, he was above the mountain lion's jump, and soon he had inched out of sight. In this way the worm crawled up and up through many sleeps for about one whole snow, and at last he reached the top.

Measuring worm picked up the bear cubs and in the same way he went up, took them safely down to the floor of the valley. Since that time, the boulder that grew to be a great high rock has been called Tu-tok-a-nu'-la in honor of Tul-tak-a-na, the measuring worm.

Measuring worm again ascended to the top of the great rock where he leaned out across the Valley of Ah-wah'-nee. He leaned out so far that he stretched across to the opposite side of the canyon with his head on one side and his tail on the other. He then crossed over to the south rim of the valley.

Later he reversed his route, recrossed to the north rim, and again descended to the floor of the valley. The walls of the canyon then began to cave in, and all the bird and animal people of Ah-wah'-nee were forced to flee down the river. In those days, the valley was much deeper than now and somewhat narrower. The caving-in of its walls partly filled the valley and made all of the earth and the piles of rocks that now make up the floor of the valley.

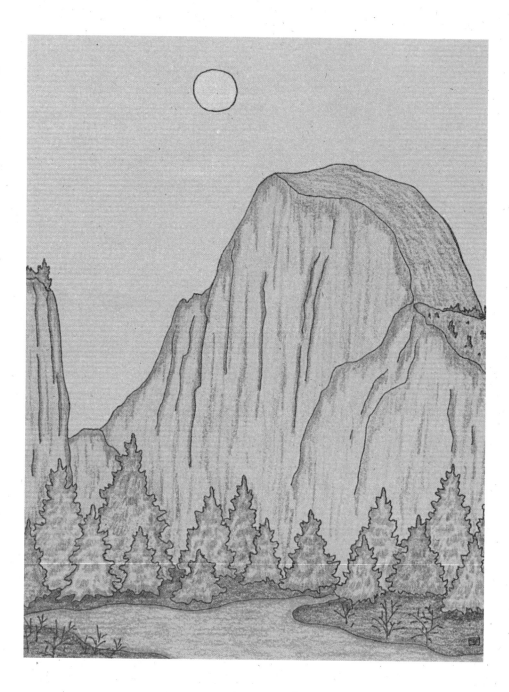

The Legend of Tis-se'-yak

A woman, Tis-se'-yak, and her husband traveled from a country very far off, and entered the Valley of Ah-wah'-nee foot-sore and weary. She walked before her husband, bowing far forward under the heavy burden of her great conical basket which was strapped across her forehead. He followed easily after her with a rude staff in his hand and a roll of animal skins flung over his back.

After their long journey across the mountains they were very thirsty, and they hurried to find cool water to drink. The woman was still in front, and so she was the first to reach the lake called A-wai'-a. She quickly dipped up the water of the lake in her basket and drank long and deep. She was so thirsty, she drank up all the water and drained the lake dry before her husband arrived.

Because the woman had drunk all the water, there came a severe drought in the Valley of Ah-wah'-nee, and the earth was dried up so that it yielded neither herb nor grass.

The woman's actions greatly displeased her husband, and his wrath was made the greater because he had no water. In his anger, he took up his staff and beat the woman soundly. She fled from him, but he pursued her and beat her more still. The woman wept and became enraged herself. She turned about and scolded her husband, then flung her basket at him.

At the very moment that they stood facing each other, the woman and her husband were turned into stone for their wickedness. There they have remained to this day. The basket lies upturned beside the husband, and the woman's rock face is stained with the long, dark lines from her tears.

The Bear and the Fawns

O-soo'-ma-te the Grizzly Bear had a sister-in-law whose name was O-woo'-yah the Deer. Grizzly Bear took Deer to a place in the woods to show her a good kind of clover. When they found the clover, Deer began to scratch her head. Grizzly Bear said, "Let me louse your head. Let me bite the lice." Grizzly Bear bit Deer so that she died, and took her liver out and put it in a basket and carried it home.

Deer had told her two Fawns before she left that a bag hung in the house. She told the Fawns, "If your aunt, Grizzly Bear, harms me, that bag will fall from where it hangs." The bag fell.

When Grizzly Bear came home, the little Fawns asked, "Aunt, where is our mother?"

Grizzly Bear replied, "She is out gathering clover."

After a little they asked, "Why doesn't mother come home?" They saw the liver in the basket and smelled it and knew it was their mother's liver. They began to cry and say, "Our mother is dead, our mother is dead."

Later the Fawns asked Grizzly Bear if they might take her Cubs and play with them. She answered, "All right, but do not hurt them."

So the Fawns took the Cubs out in the woods to play, and they found a cave. They said to the Cubs, "We will go in first and you close the hole and smoke us, and when we call, you let us out. Then you go in and we will smoke you."

The Fawns went in first and the Cubs closed the hole and made smoke go in, and when the smoke was thick the Fawns called to be let out, and the Cubs let them out. The Fawns then fanned the Cubs in the cave. The smoke became too dense and the Cubs called to the Fawns to cease. They only fanned the harder until the Cubs were suffocated.

"We had better watch out, or Grizzly Bear will kill us, too," they said to one another. They decided to leave without saying anything and to go to their grandfather, Paw'-bun-dee the Lizard. They knew that Grizzly Bear would soon come looking for them.

When the Fawns reached their grandfather's house, they told him of the terrible fate which had overtaken their mother. "Where is Grizzly Bear?" Lizard asked them. "She is following us and will soon be here," they replied. Upon hearing this, Lizard threw two large white stones into the fire and heated them.

When Grizzly Bear arrived outside of Lizard's house she could not find an entrance. She asked Lizard how she might enter. He told her to climb up on top and come in through the smoke hole, and to back down or she would fall and break her neck. Grizzly Bear did as she was instructed, for she was anxious to get the two Fawns, whom Lizard had told her were in his house. But as Grizzly Bear began to back through the smoke hole, Lizard took the red hot stones from the fire and burned her to death. Grizzly Bear rolled from the top of Lizard's house dead.

The Spirits of Cho'-lok

In the waters just below Cho'-lok (Yosemite Falls) live the Po'-loti, a group of dangerous spirit women. In the old days there was a village a short distance from the falls.

A maiden from this village went to the stream for a basket of water. She dipped the basket into the stream as usual, but brought it up full of snakes. She went farther up stream and tried again, but with the same result. She tried repeatedly, each time a little farther up stream, but always drew a basketful of snakes.

Finally, she reached the pool at the foot of Cho'-lok, and a sudden, violent wind blew her into it.

During the night she gave birth to a child which she wrapped in a blanket and brought home the next morning. The girl's mother was very curious and soon took the blanket off the baby in order to see it.

Immediately a violent gale arose and blew the entire village and its inhabitants into this same pool. Nothing has ever been seen or heard of them since.

The Spirits of Po-ho-no

In the lake from which the waters of Po-ho-no (Bridal Veil Fall) flow, lives a group of beautiful maidens. They are pure white, with blue eyes and long hair that hangs down to their feet. Possessing a very sharp sense of smell, they can detect easily the approach of a human being. They cause a violent wind to blow in an effort to carry any persons nearby into the lake to drown. The maidens then devour their victims whose spirits remain forever in the depths of the lake. Very little is known about the maidens because they are greatly feared and anyone who comes in sight of one takes no time for observation, but makes off, if possible, at top speed. Over the years, several persons have lost their lives in the lake and in the stream below it.

The waterfall, Po-ho-no, is also bewitched. Once an Indian woman was out gathering seeds a short distance above the fall, and by some mishap, she lost her balance and fell into the stream. The force of the current carried her down with such speed that before any assistance could be rendered, she was swept over the precipice, and was never seen again.

Po-ho-no has since been known as the home of an evil spirit with the breath of a fatal wind, and the fall is dreaded and shunned. Whenever a person has to pass it, he or she experiences a tremendous feeling of distress, and hurries by at the height of speed. No one will sleep near the fall, and to point at it while traveling by means certain death. The voices of all

those who have drowned in the fall can still be heard perpetually warning others to shun Po-ho-no.

A different group of supernatural beings once resided in the pool at the base of Po-ho-no. Little is known about these beings which were reportedly harmless except for their practice of causing the water of the fall to blow out and wet anyone who approached too close to its foot.

Ho-hā'-pe, the River Mermaids

Some of the rivers are inhabited by Ho-hā'-pe, the River Mermaids or Water Women. These Mermaids have long hair and are beautiful to look at. They usually live in deep pools, and are known at several places in Wah-kal'-mut-tah (the Merced River). In that part of the river that runs through the valley of Ah-wah'-nee, the River Mermaids have been seen a number of times.

One Mermaid lived down the river at the upper end of Pleasant Valley in the large round pool called Ow'-wal. In the early days, two partners used to fish for salmon at the pool, one on each side of the river. Several times they saw the River Mermaid.

Another lived in the deep water at Wel'-le-to below Pleasant Valley. At this place not long ago, some Indians from Bear Valley and Coulterville came to catch salmon. They put their net in a deep place in the river, and when it was full of fish, tried to pull it out. Try as they might, they could not free the net for it was stuck on the bottom. Ho-hā'-pe the River Mermaid had fastened the net to a rock, but the men did not know this. One of them entered the water to find where the net had caught, and to lift it up. While he was doing this, the River Mermaid put a turn of the net-rope around his big toe and he was drowned. Then several of the men had to go down to get him. After they brought up his body, all of them saw the River Mermaid in the pool below, her long hair floating out in the current.

Hoo-meh-let'-kee Travels to the Hereafter

Once in the Valley of Ah-wah'-nee there lived an old man, Hoo-meh-let'-kee, and his wife, Aw-naw-hawt'-kee. They had lived together for many years and were very much attached to each other. Their home was in the village below and east of Cho'-lok (Yosemite Falls).

One day the old wife died, and she was buried in the cemetery at the mouth of the canyon called Tah-hah-chee' (Indian Canyon). As was their custom, the bird and animal people came once each day for three days to sprinkle ashes on the grave.

For three days and nights Hoo-meh-let'-kee kept watch at the grave. Early on the morning of the fourth day he heard a rumbling sound in the ground. Slowly his dead wife arose from her grave. She did not appear to recognize her husband.

Unseen by anyone but Hoo-meh-let'-kee, the risen wife remained about the village all day. At nightfall she climbed the old trail up the canyon called Tah-hah-chee' and began walking west.

The old man followed her closely, but his wife would not look back. She put a shawl over her head and kept her face turned from him. As the sun was beginning to rise, the couple came to a cave on the mountain. The woman entered the cave and Hoo-meh-let'-kee followed her. But when they had entered the dark cave, the husband could not see his dead wife

anymore. She had disappeared.

Hoo-meh-let'-kee searched for his dead wife and grieved for a long time.

Finally, the old man met the keeper of the gate to the Hereafter and asked to be let in. He was told that he was not dead and that he would smell bad to the dead people. They talked for a long time, but at last the husband convinced the keeper to allow him to enter.

Following the trail over which his dead wife had gone, Hoo-meh-let'-kee caught up with her just as she came to a very narrow and rickety bridge across a river. The bridge was smooth and slippery, but the dead wife crossed it without trouble. Close behind, Hoo-meh-let'-kee was able to cross also, and followed his dead wife on toward the west.

After a long journey, the dead wife turned and spoke to her husband. She said, "You must not follow me any farther. You are not dead and you will smell bad to the dead people. I must go to my people who have died and stay with them. You go back to our village and stay there until you die. Then you can come up and be with me."

When Hoo-meh-let'-kee arrived at the Hereafter, he saw many of his people who had died long before. Some of these were black because their bodies had been burned after they had died. The rest bore their natural color.

The keeper of the Hereafter told the old man that he could not stay and took him back across the bridge and to the mouth of the cave where he could find his way home. When Hoo-meh-let'-kee arrived home he told his people of his travels, and that is how they came to know about the Hereafter.

The Birth of Wek'-wek

Yayil the Condor always roosted on a large rock on a small hill between the west bank of the San Joaquin river and the eastern foot of Mount Diablo. He flew about hunting, but always returned every night to roost on this rock.

After a time, the rock became ill, and Condor brought two doctors to cure her. The doctors at once began to gather wood. It took them a whole day to bring enough for their purpose. That night they built a big fire and placed the rock in its center. Then they piled on still more wood.

When the rock became very hot, it suddenly burst with a loud bang, and from it came Wek'-wek the Falcon. As he emerged, he gave his characteristic cry, "wek." Falcon flew to a tree and alighted upon a branch. The doctors told Condor that his wife was well and had given birth to a boy.

Falcon straightaway became chief. He noticed that whenever he flew about, all the rocks called after him, "oooooo." One day Falcon asked his father, "Why is it that all the rocks shout at me whenever I go out?" "Oh," said Condor, "those are your relatives. They are rejoicing that you are chief."

The next day as Falcon flew near the river, he heard the shouting from the rocks and decided to sit on a stump and watch. He noticed an object moving up and down the river, making a large ripple. He went to his

father and inquired about this strange being.

Condor said, "My son, that is your grandfather, the biggest and wisest man in the world." "Well," said Falcon, "I wish I might get him out of the water where I could talk to him and learn something." Condor replied, "That you could never do. You might catch him and cut a small piece from his body. That would then come to life and talk to you."

Next day the boy took his stone knife and sat down to watch for his grandfather. Finally, he cut off a piece of the stump upon which he was sitting, brought it home and left it in the house.

The next morning Ah-hā'-le the Coyote appeared and walked around the house. Condor then said, "Now, my son, you have your grandfather, and he can instruct you in many things. I, myself, know very little. Of course, I will help you as much as possible, but Coyote can tell you all you wish to know." Coyote agreed to help Falcon make anything he desired.

Falcon then went everywhere, and Coyote answered all his questions about things he had seen.

Wek'-wek's Contest with Ki'-lak

Wek'-wek the Falcon was talking with his grandfather, Ah-hā'-le the Coyote. He said, "Now, grandfather, I want to have a good time, so I am going to see Ki'-lak, of whom you have told me." Coyote replied, "All right, but you must be very careful." Falcon said, "Well, I will, of course, be careful, but I want to play a game with Ki'-lak." Coyote's parting warning was to be very cautious and to have plenty of beads with which to gamble. When Falcon started, great quantities of beads came flying after him.

When he reached Ki'-lak's house, Falcon said, "I have come to see you. I want to visit and play games with you." Ki'-lak agreed to play later, saying that he did not feel well just then.

Now Ki'-lak had a big dance house built entirely of stone. He made a great hot fire and put into it eight round stones each about the size of a child's head. These were the stones with which they were to play. Ki'-lak suggested that Falcon take first chance in the game. After some discussion, it was agreed that Ki'-lak should be the first to try his skill at dodging. Ki'-lak flew, therefore, constantly singing as is the custom of the one who is doing the "dodging" in any game. Falcon threw eight stones but missed the mark each time. He did not want to kill Ki'-lak yet, so purposely missed him. Coyote had told Falcon before he left home that if he wished to kill Ki'-lak he must strike a small, white spot on the under surface of the

59

right wing. Here was located Ki'-lak's heart, his only vulnerable spot.

Next, Ki'-lak threw at Falcon with no better success. The two again exchanged places with like results.

Finally, while Ki'-lak was throwing for the fourth time, he began to fear that Falcon might yet beat him.

Then, as Falcon was throwing at Ki'-lak in this fourth series, he said to himself, "This is really easy. I can kill this fellow any time I like."

Falcon's grandfather, Ah-wahn'-dah the Turtle, lived here with Ki'-lak. He prompted Falcon at this point, saying, "You had better kill that fellow. Hit his heart, right at the small white spot."

Now before leaving for his journey to visit Ki'-lak, Falcon had placed a single condor feather on top of the house of Mol'-luk the Condor as a life token. He had arranged that if he were killed, the feather was to fall over; if he were ill or in danger, it was to sway.

Falcon had missed Ki'-lak so often by now that he despaired of success and decided to give up and let Ki'-lak hit him, thus ending the contest. He did so and fell to the ground stunned. Ki'-lak thought that Falcon was dead and threw him aside in a corner of the house.

Just then the feather on Condor's house fell, and Coyote knew what had happened. He wept bitterly and rolled about on the ground in his sorrow. Finally, he rose and started off to see Ki'-lak.

Coyote told Ki'-lak, "I am an old man. I have come here to play with you, and we will have a hard game." Then they laid their wagers and began to play. Because of Coyote's rage and desire for vengeance, he missed the first four shots he took. However, his fifth stone struck the small white spot on Ki'-lak's wing and killed him instantly.

When Ki'-lak died, everything throughout the world appeared to burst open. Almost immediately, the whole world began to burn. It burned a very long time. As the fire neared the point where Coyote lay he said to Falcon, "Take you sister and go down to the ocean and into the water until the world cools off. Condor and I will remain here. Nothing can harm us."

After about a month the world was sufficiently cool for Falcon to return. Coyote asked him how he had fared down in the ocean. Falcon replied that he had been very comfortable.

Wek'-wek's Visit to the Underworld People

Wek'-wek the Falcon was digging holes in the sand to find roots and seeds that were good to eat. In digging, he came to a very deep hole which led down under the world. Falcon went down this hole, and when he reached the underworld, he found other people there. He took a wife with a little boy. Besides his new wife there were To-to'-kon the Sandhill Crane, Wah'-ah the Heron, Cha-poo'-kah-lah the Blackbird, and others.

Sandhill Crane was chief. When he saw Falcon he said, "What shall we do with this visitor? He is lost. We had better kill him."

Falcon watched a man make ready with his bow and arrow, so Falcon invited him to come and eat. The man came and ate, and when his belly was full went back to Sandhill Crane.

The chief said, "I did not send you to eat, but to kill Falcon." Then he sent another, and Falcon asked him also to come and eat, and he did as the other had done. Then Sandhill Crane sent two men together to kill him, but Falcon called them both to come and eat. They did so. Then Sandhill Crane was angry. He sent no more men, but went himself, taking his bow and arrow.

Falcon said to him, "Come in," whereupon Sandhill Crane shot his arrow. It missed its mark.

Then Falcon came out and faced the underworld people. They fired all

their arrows but could not kill him. Falcon said, "You cannot kill me with arrows. Have you a pot big enough to hold me?"

"Yes," they answered.

"Then set it up and put me in it," he said.

And they did as they were told and put Falcon in the hot pot and put the cover on. When he was burned, they took out his burnt bones and buried them in the ground.

Ah'-ut the Crow, Falcon's nephew, missed his uncle, and went to his uncle's partner, Hoo-loo'-e the Dove, who was in the hole crying. Crow asked where Falcon had gone. Dove pointed down the hole. Crow went down and found the rancheria of the underworld people and killed them all. He then asked Falcon's new wife where her husband had gone. She answered that the people had burned and buried him.

Falcon stayed in the ground five days and then came to life. He came out and asked his wife where the underworld people were. She told him that Crow had come and killed them all. "That is too bad," he exclaimed. "I wanted to show them what kind of man I am." Then Falcon said that she should stay there and he would take the boy and go home.

She answered, "All right."

Then he shot an arrow up through the hole that had brought him to the underworld, and caught hold of it. He held the boy tightly, and the arrow carried them both back to the upper world.

Sources And Notes

1. Ū-wū'-lin, the Giant of Ah-wah'-nee

This is the first of six different legends regarding the peopling of the world. It is taken from Barrett's *Myths of the Southern Sierra Miwok* (p. 2). In that work, Barrett combined five such legends in one long narrative (the story of the fifth peopling was never recorded). For this work, we have separated that narrative into the five legends which begin the book. Barrett used the spelling "Ū-wū'-lin," which name signifies eater and is derived from "u'wu," to eat.

Other versions of the legend appear in Merriam (1910), page 169; in Gifford and Block (1930), p. 94; in Latta (1936), page 121; and in Broadbent (1964), p. 173. Interesting variations include a burning of the dead giant's body and the heroic act of a bird who recovered the giant's escaped eye (Merriam), the location of the death in Coulterville where the giant's immense petrified bones were later discovered by a man who died within a few days of digging them up (Gifford and Block), and the addition by Chris Brown that the jerky which the giant left drying on a rock near the Cascades in Yosemite Valley still hangs to this day (Latta).

2. Yel'-lo-kin, the Man-Eating Giant

The second legend about the peopling of the world is from Merriam's *Dawn of the World* (p. 163). Other versions can be found in Barrett (1919), p. 3, and Gifford and Block (1930), p. 95. Both of these alternate forms indicate that the second race of people was eliminated by big black ants that overran the world.

3. How Kah'-kool the Raven Became a Great Hunter

This story about raven learning to hunt and assuming his black coloration appears in Merriam's *Dawn of the World* (p. 93). Some of its repetitive sections have been omitted. Merriam identifies the animals' home as Bower Cave (as does Barrett).

Other versions are included in Barrett (1919), p. 3, and Gifford and Block (1930), p. 95. Barrett reports that the chiefs of the the third group of people were Morning-star and Puma. Gifford and Block's account notes that when the people who resided in the cave abandoned it, the great quantity of food they left hardened and turned into the stalactites and stalagmites still found in the cave.

4. The Greed of His'-sik the Skunk

This legend about skunk's vanity and greed might be considered a Yosemite Miwok morality tale. It, too, comes from Merriam's *Dawn of the*

World (p. 117). The food "pinole" referred to in the legend is flour made from grass seeds.

Other forms of the legend can be found in Barrett (1919), p. 3, and Gifford and Block (1930), p. 96. Barrett's version concludes by adding that following the feast each character assumed the particular animal form it has now, and that none had to hunt again with bow and arrow.

5. How Ah-hā'-le Created People

The last of the legends concerning the peopling of the world is taken from Barrett's *Myths of the Southern Sierra Miwok* (p. 4).

Similar versions appear in Merriam (1910), p. 61; Kroeber (1907), p. 202; Wilson (1923), p. 17; and Gifford and Block (1930), p. 97. Kroeber's account is quite abbreviated and is limited to Duck diving for mud to create the earth. Wilson's largely unauthentic rendition is considerably embellished and romanticized, and it adds the tale of White-footed Mouse stealing fire and a variation on Coyote planting feathers to make people.

6. How Ah-hā'-le Stole the Sun for the Valley People

The importance of the sun is reflected in the number of Native American legends about it which have been collected in California. This Mariposa-area Miwok story appears in Merriam's *Dawn of the World* (p. 35) and incorporates some aspects of the same story recounted by Barrett in *Myths of the Southern Sierra Miwok* (p. 19).

Additional versions are to be found in Kroeber (1907), p. 202; Wilson (1923), p. 18; Broadbent (1964), p. 169; and Freeland (1982), p. 102. Kroeber's legend discusses the fact that neither the Chukchansi Yokuts nor the Monos received fire, and as a result, the Monos cannot speak well because they are too cold. He also adds a short paragraph about how life changed for Coyote and his people after they obtained fire. Wilson's account is very short, and probably fictitious or taken from a non-local legend. He attributes the theft of fire to White-footed Mouse. Some of the fire that Mouse brought back shot up into the sky and became the sun, and some of it remained in the trees. Ever since then people have known that by rubbing the sticks of buckeye or cedar together they can make fire.

7. How Meadowlark Started Death

Many California Indian groups passed down legends which explain why people die. This example from the Pohonichi Miwok (what anthropologists called the Southern Miwok at one time) is taken from Kroeber's *Indian Myths of South Central California* (p. 203). It was told among the Chukchansi Yokuts by Bill White and Captain Charlie, both half Southern Miwok and half Chukchansi Yokuts in descent.

Other versions are included in Merriam (1910), p. 55; Kroeber (1923), p. 70; and Gifford and Block (1930), p. 126. Kroeber's later telling of the legend indicates that Coyote originally planned to cover the dead with blankets for four days to have them arise reborn in the prime of manhood. This worked well until Meadowlark, who was newly married, became dis-

turbed during his honeymoon by the odors of decay emanating from the blanket-covered pile. In the interest of marital bliss, Meadowlark convinced Coyote to burn the dead, eliminate the foul odor, and end the practice of repeatedly renewing human life.

8. Tim-me-lā'-le the Thunder

This story about the origin of thunder and rain develops interestingly from the Giant of Ah-wah'-nee legend. It is taken from Merriam's *Dawn of the World* (p. 173).

No similar versions were located, but variations are included in Kroeber (1907), p. 203, and Latta (1936), p. 111. These two "Bear and Fawns" legends end with the young deer becoming two forms of thunder with supernatural powers.

9. The Legend of Tu-tok-a-nu'-la

In this collection, this is the first legend in which a major Yosemite Valley landmark (El Capitan, in this instance) is integral to the story. It appears in *Tribes of California* by Stephen Powers (p. 366); his spelling is used. He relied on Choko (also known as "Old Jim") for his information. Powers called the legend "a true Indian story" and "a kind of parallel to the fable of the hare and the tortoise." The second portion of the legend describing how the floor of Yosemite Valley came to be filled with rock comes from Barrett's *Myths of the Southern Sierra Miwok* (p. 22).

A number of other versions of the El Capitan legend have been recorded including those in Clark (1904), p. 92; Barrett (1919), p. 22; Wilson (1923), p. 104; Gifford and Block (1930), p. 264; Latta (1936), p. 107; Brown (1941), p. 25; and Broadbent (1964), p. 161. Clark substitutes boys for the bear cubs. In many renditions, the bear cubs are accompanied by their mother. In Brown, the stranded creatures are moles who rested on the flat rock following an exhausting football game. In Broadbent, another green measuring worm sits on El Capitan as it grows. A major variation that recurs in the literature has the bears perishing atop the cliff. When the measuring worm returns from the summit, he carries only their bones.

10. The Legend of Tis-se'-yak

This colorful story is also taken from *Tribes of California* by Powers (p. 367), and utilizes his spelling. An earlier version of the legend called "Tu-tock-ah-nu-lah and Tis-sa-ack" appeared in *Hutchings' California Magazine* (Nov., 1859), and in his *Scenes of Wonder of Curiosity in California* (p. 103), but Powers called it "a production quite too embellished to have originated in a California Indian's imagination...it is not representative, not illustrative." He attributed the Hutchings account to S. M. Cunningham, one of the earliest settlers in the valley. Clark (1904), p. 78, reprinted this discredited version.

The rock figures mentioned in the legend are Half Dome (which represents the woman's head), North Dome (her husband), and Basket Dome (her upturned basket). Lake A-wai'-a is now called Mirror Lake. Powers

noted that for the Yosemite Miwok, the "acme of female beauty is reached in the fashion of cutting off the hair straight across the top of the forehead, and allowing the side-locks to droop beside the ears." Apparently the Indians were able to perceive this square-cut female appearance on the face of Half Dome (along with the black stains from the woman's tears).

Many other versions of the legend have been published. In addition to the Hutchings rendition, there are variant forms in Clark (1904), p. 87; Barrett (1919), p. 21; Wilson (1923), p. 79; Gifford and Block (1930), p. 263; and Latta (1936), p. 125. Most of them are more elaborate and account for the origin of additional Yosemite Valley landmarks. In Barrett, for example, the woman also carried a finely feathered basket full of seeds and a baby on its cradle board. Her husband beat her with a white oak club. The seeds were planted and established the variety of plant foods that exists in Yosemite Valley. The cradle board was thrown against the valley's north wall and now appears as the Royal Arches, the husband's club was discarded and became a snag in Mirror Lake, and the husband himself became Washington Column.

11. The Bear and the Fawns

This commonly recorded legend appears in a form created by combining versions from Gifford's *Miwok Myths* (p. 333), Gifford and Block's *California Indian Nights' Entertainment* (p. 237), and Merriam's *Dawn of the World* (p. 111). The spelling of "Paw'-bun-dee" is from Latta.

Other versions include those in Kroeber (1917), p. 203; Wilson (1923), p. 123; Latta (1936), p. 111; Broadbent (1964) p. 177; de Angulo (1976), p. 69; and Freeland (1982), p. 98. In several accounts, Grizzly Bear is directed to back down (or sit on) the fire hole atop Lizard's home, and a hot fire rock is forced into her vagina, burning her to death. This is the version reported to Craig Bates by Agnes Castro, who learned it from her grandparents, Captain and Suzie Sam. Another variation finds the fawns, after Grizzly Bear dies, ascending into the sky and becoming thunder.

12. The Spirits of Cho'-lok

The first of three stories about water spirits, this legend comes from Barrett's *Myths of the Southern Sierra Miwok* (p. 23). He indicates that women-spirits similar to those above Bridal Veil Fall (see "The Spirits of Po-ho-no") are also in the waters that flow into Yosemite Falls.

An almost identical version appears in Gifford and Block (1930), p. 265. Latta (1936), p. 129, presents a similar account as part of the Lost Arrow legend which he learned from Chris Brown.

13. The Spirits of Po-ho-no

This legend combines early information from *Scenes of Wonder and Curiosity* by Hutchings (p. 108) with the account of Barrett in *Myths of the Southern Sierra Miwok* (p. 23). Both men discuss the lake "thirteen miles" above Bridal Veil Fall upon which a strong wind blows. This is present-day

Ostrander Lake which is the source of Bridal Veil Creek.

In a later version of the legend, Hutchings (1886) suggests that the "superstition" about Bridal Veil Fall grew out of a natural phenomenon: invariably a "peculiar and strong wind" blows within a radius of about a half mile of the fall (p. 406). He adds that the legend may also have evolved to keep persons away from the danger presented by the slippery, moss-lined pools at the top of the fall.

Similar forms of the legend appear in Smith (1904), p. 13, and Wilson (1923), p. 116. The Smith version is decorated considerably, while Wilson's account is only slightly embroidered. Clark (1904), p. 95, tells the legend of Grouse Lake (in the south section of Yosemite near Wawona) about the spirit of a drowned Indian boy which cries (like "a puppy when lost") to warn others away from meeting a similar fate in the lake.

14. Ho-hā'-pe, the River Mermaids

This, a third account of water-related beings, is taken from Merriam's *Dawn of the World* (p. 228). He characterized the story as a "present day myth." Similar river mermaids occur in the legends of Indian groups up and down the state. Pleasant Valley now lies beneath the waters of man-made Lake McClure.

Wilson (1923), p. 125, provides a slightly romanticized version of the fish women.

15. Hoo-meh-let'-kee Travels to the Hereafter

This story of death and the afterlife is taken from Latta's *California Indian Folklore* (p. 117), and was told by Chris Brown. Originally titled "The Orpheus of Yosemite," it has been located in no other source. The spellings used are those of Latta. The cave that the old man and his wife entered is probably Bower Cave, near Bull Creek, northeast of Mariposa. Chris Brown reported to Latta that all Yosemite Indians entered the "Hereafter" through this cave.

16. The Birth of Wek'-Wek

Kroeber (1921), p. 70, calls Wek'-wek the greatest hero of Miwok legends, and indicates that the "Miwok never tire of telling about this character, who impersonates all that they conceive of daring and magic and skill in the days of long ago." Merriam (1910) characterized Wek'-wek as a divinity with supernatural powers or magic enabling him to perform miracles. This first of three Wek'-wek legends included here is taken from Barrett's *Myths of the Southern Sierra Miwok* (p. 6). Barrett says that the doctors called to cure the rock were probably snapping flycatchers.

17. Wek'-wek's Contest with Ki'-lak

The story of the bird-like monster, Ki'-lak, also comes from Barrett's Myths of the *Southern Sierra Miwok* (p. 7). Merriam (1910), p. 75, includes a version of the story from the Sacramento River area which is remarkably

similar. de Angulo (1976), p. 5, relates a number of stories regarding "Gilak monsters," but none of them seem to have originated with the Sierra Miwok.

18. Wek'-wek's Visit to the Underworld People

This legend illustrates a belief in a world, different from the "upper world," located underground. It appears in Merriam's *Dawn of the World* (p. 195). No other form of the legend is known to have been recorded.

Annotated Bibliography

Barrett, Samuel A.

1919 Myths of the Southern Sierra Miwok. *University of California Publications in American Archaeology and Ethnology* 16(1): 1-28. Berkeley: The University Press.

Barrett learned these 15 myths from Southern Miwok people in the Mariposa area during the summer of 1906. Though the names of the original tellers were not included, the myths are authentic, and serve as the source of many of the legends included in this book.

Barrett, Samuel A. and Edward W. Gifford

1933 Miwok Material Culture. *Bulletin of the Public Museum of the City of Milwaukee* 2(4): 119-337. Milwaukee, Wisconsin. Reprinted by the Yosemite Association, Yosemite National Park, California.

While there are no myths or legends reproduced here, the work discusses many aspects of tangible Miwok culture, often indicating how religious belief and myth shaped that culture. A very significant volume for its wealth of detail about the

Sierra Miwok way of life.

Broadbent, Sylvia M.

1964 The Southern Sierra Miwok Language. *University of California Publications in Linguistics* 38. Berkeley.

In the course of her linguistic studies, Broadbent recorded the texts of twelve different legends and four other stories. Both the Miwok text and the English translation are included. The stories were told to her by John Lawrence, Castro Johnson and Chris Brown.

Brown, Chris (Chief Le-mee)

1941 The Legend of El Capitan. *Yosemite Nature Notes* XX(4): 25-27. Yosemite National Park: Yosemite Natural History Association.

A variant version of the El Capitan legend included in this book, it begins with an animal "football" game gone awry, and features two moles (not bear cubs).

Bunnell, Lafayette Houghton

1911 *Discovery of the Yosemite and the Indian War of 1851 Which Led to That Event.* 4th ed. Los Angeles: C. W. Gerlicher. Reprinted in 1991 by the Yosemite Association, Yosemite National Park, California.

Bunnell makes only peripheral references to Yosemite Indian legends and customs in his chronicle of the battalion that entered Yosemite Valley in 1851 in a punitive attack on the Native residents. But much of what is known about the Yosemite Miwok at that time is derived from this work.

Clark, Galen

1904 *Indians of the Yosemite Valley and Vicinity*. Yosemite Valley: Galen Clark.

As a resident of the Yosemite area for over 50 years, Clark was well-acquainted with many of the local Miwok people. He acknowledged, however, that several of the legends that he related were not of "wholly Indian origin." Sources include J.M. Hutchings (1871) and Stephen Powers, but the legends appearing here are more "picturesque" (as Clark described them) than genuine.

de Angulo, Jaime

1953 *Indian Tales*. New York: Hill and Wang.

de Angulo was a linguist who studied among Northern California Indian groups during the first third of this century. He wrote these stories for his children, drawing on his work with Indian people including Achomawi, Pomo, Lake Miwok, and Sierra Miwok. It is difficult to separate the Miwok stories from the others, although the character Kilelli is undoubtedly

based on the Joseph Killeli mentioned below. An interesting blend of California Indian folklore, it should not be considered fully authentic.

1976 *Shabegok*. Edited, with notes, by Bob Callahan. Berkeley: Turtle Island.

These stories are combined forms of legends from various sources, and have been fictionalized in many instances. de Angulo cites Joseph Killeli, a "Yosemite Miwok Bear Shaman," as the source of a group of Yosemite stories in this collection. Several of them are unique to this work.

Freeland, L. S.
1982 *Central Sierra Miwok Myths*. Reports from the Survey of California and Other Indian Languages, Report #3. No publisher information.

L. S. "Lucy" Freeland was a student in anthropology at the University of California in the late 1910s and early 1920s. She studied a number of Indian languages and cultures, eventually specializing in the Sierra Miwok, and worked with Alfred Kroeber, E. W. Gifford, and Franz Boas. She later married Jaime de Angulo, and published a number of articles and works on the Miwok and other languages. This collection was published after her death and includes several Yosemite-

related legends.

Gifford, Edward W.

1917 Miwok Myths. *University of California Publications in American Archaeology and Ethnology* 12(8). Berkeley: The University Press.

An eminent University of California anthropologist, Gifford collected these fourteen stories during 1913 and 1914 among the Central Sierra Miwok of Tuolumne County. They were told by William Fuller of Soulsbyville and Thomas Williams of Jamestown. This is an important source book, both authentic and well-documented.

Gifford, Edward W. and Gwendoline Harris Block

1930 *Californian Indian Nights' Entertainment.* Glendale: The Arthur H. Clark Company. Reprinted in 1990 as a Bison Book by the University of Nebraska Press, Lincoln, Nebraska.

An authentic and comprehensive compilation of myths and legends from all areas of California, this key work resulted from the collaboration of anthropologist Gifford, and Block, a self-taught editor in anthropology at the University of California. Written for a general readership, the stories are based upon the extensive anthropological research of a number of investigators. Includes a section of Yosemite stories.

Hutchings, James Mason

1859 The Great Yo-Semite Valley. *Hutchings' Illustrated California Magazine* IV(5): 197-99. San Francisco.

This included the first Yosemite Indian legend ever published. Alas, the elaborate "Legend of Tu-tock-ah-nu-lah and Tis-sa-ack" was almost certainly fabricated. Unfortunately, it has been passed down through the years as legitimate.

1860 *Scenes of Wonder and Curiosity in California.* New York and San Francisco: A. Roman & Co.

It was the goal of entrepreneur Hutchings to make Yosemite known to all the world. Almost half of this guidebook was devoted to a detailed description of Yosemite Valley including two Indian legends from the area. The legend of "Tu-tock-ah-nu-lah and Tis-sa-ack" was reprinted in this volume and its later editions.

1886 *In the Heart of the Sierras.* Oakland: Pacific Press House.

In this later work dedicated almost entirely to Yosemite, Hutchings reprinted the legends from *Scenes of Wonder*, adding to them the "Legend of the Lost Arrow." It, too, is almost certainly fictitious, despite the fact that it has appeared in a number of sources since.

Kroeber, A. L.

1907 Indian Myths of South Central California. *University of California Publications in American Archaeology and Ethnology* 4(4): 167-250. Berkeley: The University Press.

In this important work, Kroeber records four abbreviated myths from the Pohonichi Miwok (the name he used for the Southern Miwok) told to him by Bill White and Captain Charlie, both of whom were half Southern Miwok and half Chukchansi Yokuts in descent. They confirm the importance of "Coyote" in Miwok folklore.

1921 Indians of Yosemite. In *Handbook of Yosemite National Park*, compiled and edited by Ansel F. Hall. New York and London: G.P. Putnam's Sons. pp. 51-73

This chapter in Hall's classic *Handbook* includes several myths and legends, and indicates that "Wek'-wek" (the Falcon) was a character who figured prominently in many Miwok stories.

Latta, Frank F.

1936 *California Indian Folklore.* Shafter, CA: F.F. Latta.

An amateur California historian, Latta travelled throughout the San Joaquin Valley and its adjacent foothills to speak with story tellers from a wide variety of Native American groups. The con-

tents are arranged by subject; one chapter is devoted to Yosemite stories. Includes the names and photographs of several of the Indian people who provided Latta the legends he published.

Mayberry, Russel (West Virginia Slim)
1938 *Ramblin' Thru' Yosemite.* Self-published.

This peculiar little pamphlet includes three Yosemite Indian songs, the origins of several place names, and additional lore, all supplied by Chris Brown (Chief Le-mee).

Merriam, C. Hart
1910 *Dawn of the World: Weird Tales of the Mewan Indians of California.* Cleveland: Arthur H. Clark Company. Reprinted in 1993 as a Bison Book by the University of Nebraska Press, Lincoln, Nebraska.

Anthropologist Merriam collected these California Miwok legends from all over the state between 1890 and 1910. They are based upon interviews with Native Americans, and are well-documented and genuine. A key source book, and the most complete treatment of Sierra Miwok legends ever written.

Powers, Stephen
1877 Tribes of California. *Contributions to North American Ethnology,*

Vol. III. Department of the Interior, U.S. Geographical and Geological Survey of the Rocky Mountain Region, J.W. Powell in charge. Washington, D.C.: U.S. Government Printing Office.

A journalist by trade, Powers studied the Indians of California during 1871 and 1872. He wrote a number of articles and reports based on this work during the following several years. Despite his lack of anthropological training, his powers of observation and analysis were excellent, and this work is considered a classic of ethnography. The book marked the first time that authentic Yosemite Miwok legends (two recounted by Choko or "Indian Jim") appeared in print.

Smith, Bertha H.

1904　　*Yosemite Legends*. San Francisco: Paul Elder and Company.

This is an attractively designed and presented selection of six Yosemite legends of suspect origin. Using Hutchings (1860) as a primary source, the author demonstrated her skill at the art of turning a short, concise legend into a longwinded and romantic epic. The writing is stylized and reflects a Europeanized concept of Native American thought.

Smith, Elinor Shane

1927　　*Po-ho-no and Other Yosemite Legends*. No publisher's information.

Based upon a number of earlier books and no original research, this group of legends is greatly romanticized and includes several fabricated stories such as the amazingly prolix "Great Dog of Half Dome." It is interesting for its popular representation of Yosemite Indian culture in the 1920s.

Taylor, Katherine Ames

1926 *Lights and Shadows of Yosemite*. San Francisco: H.S. Crocker Company, Inc.

The five legends reprinted here are taken fairly faithfully from earlier sources. The first three appeared in Hutchings' two books, and the others are based primarily on Powers (with some embellishment).

1948 *Yosemite Trails and Tales*. Stanford: Stanford University Press.

The legends reproduced here are the same ones that appeared in the author's earlier work, and reflect only minor changes.

Townsend, George Elliott

1903 *Indian Mythology of Yosemite Valley*. Overland Monthly XLI(6): 454-459.

A popular-style article, it includes two legends of questionable authenticity. The Po-ho-no story is fairly true to Hutchings' first

telling, but it has been embroidered with spurious additions. The legend of Tis-sa-ack and Tu-tock-a-nu-lah is poor creative writing. Interesting as a curiosity, but weak source material.

Wilson, Herbert Earl

1923 *The Lore and Lure of Yosemite.* San Francisco: Sunset Press.

This "popularized" collection of ten legends was distilled from a variety of sources. Some of them are reliable, others not. Despite the fact that Wilson aggregated a number of key stories, the reader would be better served to consult more original works. Although a number of different editions of this book were published, there appear to be no changes to the included legends over the years.

Contributors

Frank La Pena

Frank La Pena is Director of Native American Studies, California State University, Sacramento, where he is also a Professor of Art and Ethnic Studies.

He has written two poetry collections, *The Gift of Singing* and *Sunsa Stopped the Rain,* under his Wintu tribal name, Tauhindauli. His work has been included in several anthologies, including *CALAFIA: The California Poetry* and *The World Is a Gift,* and he wrote the chapter on Wintu people that appears in the Smithsonian Institution's *Handbook of American Indians.*

La Pena has exhibited his art work widely in the United States, Europe, Cuba and South America in one-man and group shows, winning numerous honors and awards. He is a Regional Director for the International Native American Council of Arts, a commissioner for the California Historic State Capitol Commission, and a singer/dancer who frequently participates in Northern California traditional Indian ceremonies and activities.

Born in San Francisco, La Pena lives in Sacramento.

Craig D. Bates

Craig D. Bates is Curator of Ethnography for the National Park Service Museum in Yosemite National Park. A fifth-generation Californian, he developed his deep interest in Native American cultures as a small child.

Bates acquired most of his knowledge of traditional ways from tribal elders throughout California. The late Henry Azbill, of the Maidu village of *Mikchopdo,* was a particularly close mentor. Bates has studied museum and archival collections across the country, is the author of more than 90 articles on Native American culture, and co-authored the award-winning *Tradition & Innovation: A Basket History of the Indians of the Yosemite-Mono Lake Area.*

Residing just outside Yosemite National Park, Bates practices many traditional arts, including basketry and featherwork. Items he has made are in museum and private collections, and are used by native people. His son, Carson, shares his active interest in Miwok culture.

Steven P. Medley

Steven P. Medley has served as the President of the Yosemite Association since 1985. He has worked for over fifteen years in Yosemite National Park at a variety of jobs. Much of his knowledge of Native American mythology was gained during his time as Research Librarian in the park.

Medley is the author of *The Complete Guidebook to Yosemite National Park,* has contributed to and edited a number of other Yosemite publications,

and is the editor of *Yosemite,* the quarterly journal of the Yosemite Association.

Medley resides with his wife and three boys in Oakhurst, California.

Harry Fonseca

Artist Harry Fonseca is of mixed Portuguese, Hawaiian and Nisenan-Maidu descent. He was born in 1946 and grew up in the Sacramento area, studying art at the California State University there. Fonseca has accumulated a broad knowledge of Maidu lore and traditions, much of it from his uncle, the late Henry Azbill from the Maidu village of *Mikchopdo.*

Fonseca is considered to be among the foremost native California artists. While well-known for his interpretations of Coyote mythology, he has worked in a variety of other styles. His interest in Native American rock art has inspired a number of his recent works.

The art work of Harry Fonseca has been exhibited throughout the United States and internationally, including one-man shows at such places as the Heard Museum, the Southwest Museum, and the Smithsonian Institution.

The father of one daughter, Sarah, Fonseca resides in Santa Fe, New Mexico, where he recently opened his own gallery.

Legends of the Yosemite Miwok

Designed by Michael Osborne Design, San Francisco.
Type composition in Baskerville.
Printed on 70# Simpson Evergreen and jacketed in 80# Simpson
Equinox by Phelps-Schaefer Litho-Graphics,
Brisbane, California.